WHILE YOU WAIT FOR YOUR
Prodigal

A 30-DAY PRAYER CHALLENGE

© 2024 *Revive Our Hearts* Ministries
Published by *Revive Our Hearts* Ministries
P.O. Box 2000, Niles, MI 49120

ISBN: 978-1-959704-09-6

Printed in the United States of America.

All rights reserved. No part of this publication may be reproduced in any form without permission from the publisher, except in the case of brief quotations embodied in other works or reviews.

Edited by Mindy Kroesche and Mindi Stearns.

Designed by Austin Collins.

Unless otherwise noted, all Scripture quotations are taken from the Christian Standard Bible®, Copyright © 2017 by Holman Bible Publishers. Used by permission. Christian Standard Bible® and CSB® are federally registered trademarks of Holman Bible Publishers.

Scripture quotations marked ESV are from The ESV® Bible (The Holy Bible, English Standard Version®), copyright © 2001 by Crossway, a publishing ministry of Good News Publishers. Used by permission. All rights reserved.

All emphasis in Scripture quotations has been added by the author.

CONTENTS

DAY 1   Your Sheep Has a Shepherd 7

DAY 2   A Suffering Savior (Grace Note) 13

DAY 3   The Comfort of a Rejected Savior 17

DAY 4   Let Jesus Carry It All 23

DAY 5   Don't Take It Personally 29

DAY 6   Grace Is the Antidote to Resentment 35

DAY 7   Pray It, Don't Say It 41

DAY 8   Jesus Is Praying with You 47

DAY 9   All You Need (Grace Note) 53

DAY 10   One Thing I Still Want? 57

DAY 11   Someone Is Missing from the Green Pasture 63

DAY 12   God's Grace Is Now and Forever 69

DAY 13   As Long As Jesus Is Near 75

DAY 14   God's Plan Is Much, Much Better 81

DAY 15   He Will Follow When You Can't 87

DAY 16   The Hope-Filled Promises of God (Grace Note) 93

WHILE YOU WAIT FOR YOUR *Prodigal*

DAY 17	Far Greater Than Fiction	97
DAY 18	Bring Them Home	103
DAY 19	Unmasking the Wolves	109
DAY 20	A Covenant of Peace	115
DAY 21	The Nearness of God in Your Need	121
DAY 22	"You Are My Sheep"	127
DAY 23	Rest In the Good Shepherd (Grace Note)	133
DAY 24	There's a Thief on the Loose	137
DAY 25	For Abundant Life, Enter Here	143
DAY 26	Jesus Knew Then What He Knows Now	149
DAY 27	Unsnatchable	155
DAY 28	Equipped for Adversity	161
DAY 29	Across the Jordan	167
DAY 30	He'd Leave the 99	173
	Author Bios	176

Day 1

YOUR SHEEP HAS A SHEPHERD

INTRODUCTION

by Erin Davis

On a bitter-cold, colorless day we awoke to find our sheep scattered. Most mornings we can find the flock happily grazing together in the fields behind our house. This morning was different—terribly different. A sunrise attack by a vicious predator left many of our sheep maimed. Even the ones who weren't physically hurt seemed traumatized. Just the evening before, they gladly ran toward us, their shepherds, for a treat and a nuzzle, but not now. **It was as if they'd never heard our voices before.**

One ewe in particular broke my heart. Her legs had been nipped, and she would quickly recover, but the stress of the attack left her frozen. She refused to come into the safety of the barn for warmth and care. We tried everything: speaking sweetly, a bucket full of her favorite grain, rubbing her white ears while saying, "You're okay, girl." Still, she would not move. The attack animals were still on the loose. She was in grave danger, *but her heart was stubborn*. There was nothing, it seemed, we could do.

You're taking this challenge because you love a prodigal. **Someone special to you is rebelling against the authority of God in their life and likely rejecting your influence and affection along the way**. Prodigals are not a modern phenomenon (see Gen. 3), but a shift seems to have occurred. Here at *Revive Our Hearts*, we've been inundated by messages from heartbroken parents and grandparents who are desperate to see rebellious hearts revived. **This challenge is a response to your outcry, because we believe in the power of God's Word to sustain you and the power of prayer to bring your prodigal home.**

You'll notice the theme of sheep and shepherds woven throughout this devotional. Our hope is that God's Word will help align your heart with His. For "when [Jesus] saw the crowds, he felt compassion for them, because they were distressed and dejected, like sheep without a shepherd" (Matt. 9:36).

Much like the literal sheep standing in the pasture on my little farm, your prodigal has an enemy. That enemy relentlessly seeks to steal, kill, and destroy the people God has made (John 10:10). It's no wonder, then, that your loved one (young or old) is behaving like my injured ewe: tuning out the Shepherd's voice, ignoring the pleas of those who love them most, determined to resist all that is good. Yet Jesus sees them through eyes of compassion. You are not alone in your longing to see them turn from their rebellion and run toward His loving arms.

The wait can be excruciating, the worry at times crippling, but you are not left powerless. You can pray with the assurance that:

- God hears you (1 John 5:14).
- God cares about you and your prodigal (1 Pet. 5:7).
- God doesn't want your prodigal to perish (2 Pet. 3:9).
- God is interceding with you for your wayward one (Heb. 7:25).
- God specializes in turning hearts of stone into hearts soft toward Him (Ezek. 36:26).

This is an invitation to surrender your prodigal into the loving and capable hands of his or her heavenly Father.

The challenge is this: commit to pray for your prodigal every day for the next thirty days. You'll also be asked to recruit others to pray along the way. Make a record of your requests before God. Pour out your hurt and anger and fear. Let God do the heart-work of helping you see the situation through the lens of His sovereign goodness.

Throughout these thirty days, you'll spend time each day lingering in God's Word. You'll park in four primary Scripture passages, all with something to say about the Good Shepherd and the sheep that sometimes run toward spiritual danger. You won't find easy answers or quick solutions. You will be reminded that God is willing and able to do a miraculous work in the heart of your loved one. Along the way, we've also given you "Grace Notes." These are intended to provide extra margin for you to reflect and pray for your prodigal.

As the name of our ministry implies, we believe God can revive hearts—even your prodigal's, *even yours*. Your Shepherd is speaking today. Run toward His voice as you wait for your prodigal to come home.

We believe God
can revive hearts—
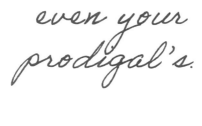

Day 2

A SUFFERING SAVIOR (GRACE NOTE)

by Ashley Gibson

TODAY'S READING: Isaiah 53:3–4

He was despised and rejected by men,
a man of suffering who knew what sickness was.
He was like someone people turned away from;
he was despised, and we didn't value him.

Yet he himself bore our sicknesses,
and he carried our pains;
but we in turn regarded him stricken,
struck down by God, and afflicted.
—Isaiah 53:3–4

You have a Savior who is able to sympathize with your heartache. He's familiar with feeling despised and rejected. He knows the sting of suffering and the ache of grief. He carried your pain. You don't have to bear it all on your own. **Give your heavy burden to Jesus. He understands its weight and He is qualified to carry it.**

A SUFFERING SAVIOR (GRACE NOTE)

You have a Savior who *is able to sympathize* with your heartache.

Day 3

THE COMFORT OF A REJECTED SAVIOR

by Erin Davis

TODAY'S READING: Isaiah 53:1–3

YOUR CHALLENGE:
Follow Jesus' lead when it comes to responding to rejection.

> He was despised and rejected by men,
> a man of suffering who knew what sickness was.
> He was like someone people turned away from;
> he was despised, and we didn't value him.
> —Isaiah 53:3

All these years later, it still makes my heart warm: that magical morning when I tiptoed into the nursery to pick up my baby and found him sitting, arms wide open and ready to hug my neck. By that point in each boy's life, I'd reached for him a zillion times but his tiny arms weren't developed enough to reach back. The moment when we could embrace each other is a metaphor for how I'd hoped our relationship would always look. *But not every parenting moment feels like a sweet snuggle.* My sons have turned away from me plenty. As painful as that can be, it's merely a shadow of a deeper ache. When the prophet Isaiah was given Spirit-filled lenses to see Jesus, he wrote, "He was like someone people turned away from" (Isa. 53:3).

Jesus knows rejection. As He spread His arms wide on the cross to rescue His beloved, He knew our arms would be too crippled by sin to reach back, "for all have sinned and fall short of the glory of God" (Rom. 3:23). And yet Jesus kept reaching. He did not withhold His love from those who spat upon Him. He didn't change His mind about redeeming those who mocked Him. He doesn't answer every rejection with fire and brimstone from heaven.

He keeps loving.
He keeps sacrificing.
He keeps pursuing.
Figuratively speaking, He keeps His arms wide open.

If your prodigal has rejected you, take comfort in knowing that Jesus has felt that particular sting. If they've rejected Jesus, too, follow His lead. Don't turn away, turn toward. Don't withdraw, welcome in. Don't go numb, keep loving. Don't cross your arms in defensiveness, open them wide. Join your heart with Jesus and dare to long for a day when your child reaches back.

PRAY

Jesus, thank You for enduring the sting of rejection for my sake. As I face rejection or apathy from the child I love, help me to love them like You love them. Lord, turn their heart toward You. They need You. I need You. Amen.

MAKE IT PERSONAL

Meditate on Isaiah 53:1–3 today. Linger on what Jesus endured for your sake.

Look up Lamentations 3:31–33. How does this passage give you hope for your prodigal?

DIG DEEPER

If you're struggling with the sting of rejection, check out "When You've Been Canceled" from the archives of the *Revive Our Hearts* blog. Here's a sneak peek: "If you've been canceled, follow the way of Christ by rehearsing blessings instead of curses in your mind for the one who rejected you. Pray for more than your comfort. Pray for the Lord to give gifts to the one who has given you sorrow."

THE COMFORT OF A REJECTED SAVIOR

Jesus knows rejection

and yet He kept reaching. He did
not withhold His love from those
who spat upon Him.

Day 4

LET JESUS CARRY IT ALL

by Erin Davis

TODAY'S READING: Isaiah 53:4

YOUR CHALLENGE:

Make a list of all you are carrying today. Surrender that list to Jesus.

> Yet he himself bore our sicknesses,
> and he carried our pains;
> but we in turn regarded him stricken,
> struck down by God, and afflicted.
> —Isaiah 53:4

Though I was too exhausted to know it at the time, holding my babies was a profound gift. As I nursed them in the night, the bottom of my rocking chair creaked back and forth. My sons are much older now. Most of them tower above me. They're harder to hold. It puts a lump in my throat just to think about it. Carrying someone is intimate, a behavior reserved for our most sacred relationships.

Your prodigal child is probably too big for you to hold too. The sweetness of the memories of snuggling them close may feel sour in light of your current relationship. I'm sure a part of you longs to put a ladder to their window, tiptoe inside and nestle in beside them. But while your intimacy with your child may be strained, for now, your intimacy with Jesus need not be. **Jesus didn't just carry the weight of your sin to the cross, He carried your sorrows too.** "Yet he himself bore our sicknesses, and he carried our pains" (Isa. 53:4).

He sees your worry about your prodigal and says, "Let me hold that." He sees the wounds painful words have cut into your heart and says, "Let me hold that." He sees your fear that your prodigal will never turn back to Him and says, "Let me hold that." He knows that their current sinful choices will have real consequences and He still says, "Let me hold that."

You will never have to carry this burden alone, even for one moment. Jesus is holding it all in His capable hands. He's not just holding the hurt and sorrow and fear, **He's holding you and He will never, ever let you go.**

> "I will be the same until your old age,
> and I will bear you up when you turn gray.
> I have made you, and I will carry you;
> I will bear and rescue you."
> —Isaiah 46:4

PRAY

Jesus, I cannot carry the weight of this journey on my own. It's too heavy. Help me to surrender it to You and let You carry it. Amen.

MAKE IT PERSONAL

What are you "carrying" as you love a prodigal? Worry? Defeat? Heartache? Make a list, then remind yourself that only Jesus can carry this load.

Think of a time when your child let you carry them. Reflect on the sweetness of that moment as you ask the Lord to work in your relationship with your prodigal child.

DIG DEEPER

Listen to the *Revive Our Hearts* podcast episode "I Will Carry You" and hear the precious song by the same name.

He sees your worry about your prodigal and says,

"Let me hold that."

Day 5

DON'T TAKE IT PERSONALLY

by Erin Davis

TODAY'S READING: Isaiah 53:5

YOUR CHALLENGE:
Pray for your prodigal to recognize that they've sinned against a holy God.

> But he was pierced because of our rebellion,
> crushed because of our iniquities;
> punishment for our peace was on him,
> and we are healed by his wounds.
> —Isaiah 53:5

Whoever offered "don't take it personally" as parenting advice has surely never raised a child of their own. Don't they know . . . ?

- *I* carried them inside *my body.*
- *I'm* the one who made them chicken noodle soup when they were sick.
- *I'm* the one who stayed up late waiting for them to come home.
- *I'm* their mother for goodness sake.

Of course this is personal! Except . . . **no sin issue has ever been cured by me-centric thinking. When we make our child's rebellion all about us, we place ourselves in a self-centered sin pattern of our own.** In this way, the enemy of our souls kills two birds with one proverbial stone. Jesus is not indifferent to your hurt, but His Word calls you to a higher view.

After his own season of rebellion, King David wrote, "Against you—*you alone*—I have sinned and done this evil in *your sight.* So you are right when you pass sentence; you are blameless when you judge" (Psalm 51:4).

Your prodigal may have sinned against you, but their greatest offenses are against a holy God. He is justified in pronouncing swift and severe judgment toward your child's sin. Instead, He extends grace. Does your heart model His in this way? Is your prayer life focused on your child's God-directed repentance or in wanting them to see how deeply they've hurt you? Are you more fixated on the ways they've violated God's perfect law or the ways in which they've violated your trust?

Perhaps a shift is warranted. The most urgent need is not the healing of your relationship but the restoration of your prodigal to God. You are right to weep and wail over their sin, for unrepentant sinners are separated from the God who loves them (Isa. 59:2). Do you long to see them restored to fellowship with Him? Are you praying for the condition of their soul? Are you asking the Lord for revival? If not, today is the day to start.

Take heart: though we are great sinners, we have a greater Savior. He has already paid the penalty for all of your prodigal's sin. Join Him in longing for them to repent and receive His grace.

PRAY

Lord, I apologize for making this about me. As a fellow sinner, I cannot sit in judgment of my child's sin. As a holy God, only You can. Help my child see their sin and turn from it. Amen.

MAKE IT PERSONAL

To your knowledge, has your child had a moment when they understood and responded to the gospel? If not, focus your prayers there, asking the Lord to save them.

How have your attempts to call your prodigal to repentance worked in the past? Recognize that you cannot change the human heart. No amount of effort on your part can make your child see their choices as sinful.

DIG DEEPER

Pick up a copy of Nancy DeMoss Wolgemuth's *Beauty in the Broken* from the ReviveOurHearts.com store. Inside this little booklet you'll find an "Am I a Proud or Broken Person?" assessment that will help you see your own sin with fresh sobriety and equip you to pray for your prodigal to be broken before the Lord.

Day 6

GRACE IS THE ANTIDOTE TO RESENTMENT

by Erin Davis

TODAY'S READING: Isaiah 53:6

YOUR CHALLENGE:

Confess your resentment to the Lord. Ask Him to remind you of His grace toward you.

> We all went astray like sheep;
> we all have turned to our own way.
> —Isaiah 53:6

If Jesus handed you a red pen and asked you to rewrite His parable about the prodigal son, what edits would you make? Given the chance to imagine the dream scenario, you'd surely delete the part about the wayward brother. Perhaps you'd develop his character so that he has the wisdom to see that rebellion only leads to pig slop. He'd stay happy and safe at home. The father doesn't need much editing of course. His horizon-watching is a comforting picture of our heavenly Father's unshakable love for us. But what about the other son? The one who received his returned brother with resentment? The one who said,

> "Look, I have been slaving many years for you, and I have never disobeyed your orders, yet you never gave me a goat so that I could celebrate with my friends. But when this son of yours came, who has devoured your assets with prostitutes, you slaughtered the fattened calf for him." (Luke 15:29–30)

You do have the red pen to rewrite his story, you know? Because his story is your story. While your prodigal child runs in rebellion away from the Father, you've chosen to stay close to His side. And though there's a big part of you that wants more than anything to see your prodigal return, there may also be a part of you that resents what their choices have cost:

- Your peace.
- Your reputation.
- Your dreams for your family.

This challenge is meant to give you the encouragement to keep praying for the Lord to work in the heart of your prodigal. It is also an invitation for you to invite the Spirit to work in *you*.

As the older brother stood sulking, refusing to go in to the celebration for his wayward brother, he'd clearly forgotten one important thing:

> We all went astray like sheep;
> we have all turned to our own way. (Isaiah 53:6)

When you've walked closely with Jesus for a while, there is a temptation to forget who you were without Him. Scripture's reminder is that at one time we all ran away from our Shepherd and refused to follow the path of obedience. Even now, there are areas of your life you are hesitant to submit to Him. Satan is often successful at convincing us that the grass is greener on the other side of the boundaries God sets.

You are both: the prodigal son and his faithful brother, and the Father has never stopped loving you. While meditating on your own sinfulness is uncomfortable, it's an important part of loving your prodigal well. Don't forget that "the LORD has punished him for the iniquity of us all" (Isa. 53:6).

Remembering the Lord's forgiveness roots out resentment because **grace getters are grace givers.**

Instead of focusing your prayers on your prodigal today, ask the Lord to work in your heart. Invite Him to help you see yourself as the runaway sheep you once were. Thank Him anew for His profound grace.

PRAY

Father, thank You for loving me even when I run away from You. Thank You for Your grace. Help me to see my need for You with fresh awareness today. Root out all resentment in my heart. Amen.

GRACE IS THE ANTIDOTE TO RESENTMENT

MAKE IT PERSONAL

What are three words you'd use to describe yourself before giving your life to Christ? Write them down.

Sing "Amazing Grace" out loud today as a reminder that you once were lost, but now you're found. You were blind, but because of God's grace, now you can see.

DIG DEEPER

How do we shift from resentment to rejoicing? That's the question Betsy Childs Howard asks in the blog post "The Struggle of Rejoicing with Those Who Rejoice." Find it at ReviveOurHearts.com.

Day 7

PRAY IT, DON'T SAY IT

by Erin Davis

TODAY'S READING: Isaiah 53:7–9

YOUR CHALLENGE:
Resist the urge to keep talking at your prodigal. Rest in God alone.

> He was oppressed and afflicted,
> yet he did not open his mouth.
> Like a lamb led to the slaughter
> and like sheep silent before her shearers,
> he did not open his mouth.
> —Isaiah 53:7

"Pray it, don't say it." Those are the wise words once offered to me by a mom with children much older than my own.

When it comes to your prodigal, have you considered the value of holding your tongue? I'm not talking about weaponizing silence as a means of manipulation. There's nothing Christlike (or productive) about that. But rather resisting the urge to keep correcting, pleading, and explaining. Imagine turning down the volume of your voice to make space for your child to hear the voice of the Lord. If your prodigal is prone to attacking you with their words, have you resisted the urge to defend yourself and asked the Lord to be your guard?

Jesus modeled this perfectly: "He was oppressed and afflicted, yet he did not open his mouth" (Isa. 53:7).

Mark tells us in his Gospel:

> Then the high priest stood up before them all and questioned Jesus, "Don't you have an answer to what these men are testifying against you?" But he kept silent and did not answer (Mark 14:60–61).

Jesus wasn't silent because He didn't have anything worth saying. He didn't cower because His accusers were right. He wasn't too timid to stand up for truth. **He simply knew He didn't need to defend Himself. What others believed, or didn't believe, about Him couldn't depose Him from His throne.**

David sung about his Defender this way when others hurled accusations at him:

> Rest in God alone, my soul,
> for my hope comes from him.
> He alone is my rock and my salvation,
> my stronghold; I will not be shaken.
> My salvation and glory depend on God, my
>   strong rock.
> My refuge is in God. (Psalm 62:5–7)

Is your refuge in God alone, or are you busy building a fortress of words to try to protect yourself? Are you convinced that if you just said the right thing at the right time, your prodigal would see their error and turn? If so, try a different approach today. Rest in God alone. If need be, let Him defend you. **Resist the urge to keep talking at your prodigal, and direct your words toward God instead. In other words, pray it, don't say it.**

PRAY

Lord, I rest in You alone. My hope comes from You. You alone are my rock and my salvation. You are my stronghold. Because of You, I will not be shaken. Help me to remember that You are my defender. You are my rock! My refuge is in You. Amen.

MAKE IT PERSONAL

How have you used your words in the past to try to win your prodigal back to Jesus? What have been the results?

Make a commitment to pray more for your prodigal than you talk to them about their sin. Who can hold you accountable with this?

Meditate on Proverbs 10:19. Has using too many words led to sin in your relationship with your prodigal?

DIG DEEPER

Check out the *Grounded* episode "Wisdom for Parenting Adult Children with Holly Elliff, Helen Jones, and Bob Lepine." Find it at ReviveOurHearts.com/Grounded.

Day 8

JESUS IS PRAYING WITH YOU

by Erin Davis

TODAY'S READING: Isaiah 53:10–12

YOUR CHALLENGE:
Ask someone else to pray for your prodigal.

> Yet he bore the sin of many and
> interceded for the rebels.
> —Isaiah 53:12

I once met a mother whose daughter's prodigal years spanned three decades. That's a long time to wait for restoration. When I asked her what she did when she was tempted to give up hope, she told me she asked others to pray. At times she felt so desperate that she'd ask friends to come and pray in her daughter's childhood bedroom. **When she felt "prayed out," she leaned on others to cry out.**

It's part of Christ's design for His Church that we would bear each other's burdens (Gal. 6:2–5) and pray for one another (James 5:16). But even if you can't find a single prayer partner to battle beside you, **you never pray alone.**

Through the power of the Spirit, the prophet Isaiah saw ahead and knew that as Jesus hung on the cross He would cry out to the Father to forgive the prodigal-hearted:

> Therefore I will give him the many as a portion,
> and he will receive the mighty as spoil,
> because he willingly submitted to death,
> and was counted among the rebels;
> yet he bore the sin of many
> *and interceded for the rebels.* (Isaiah 53:12)

Jesus didn't stop praying after He accomplished His work on the cross. Right now, right this very moment, He is praying for you.

> Christ Jesus is the one who died, but even more, has been raised; he also is at the right hand of God and intercedes for us. (Romans 8:34)

Every time you intercede for your child, you are in a prayer circle with Jesus. He doesn't want your prodigal to perish (2 Pet. 3:9). From the throne room, He is interceding with you. What a comfort!

As you continue this 30-day journey of praying for your prodigal, invite others in. Reach out to a wise friend or two and ask them to pray specifically for your prodigal. When you do, you're not just redistributing the weight of the heavy load you're carrying, you're giving others an opportunity to be like Jesus, the One who prays for rebels.

PRAY

Jesus, thank You for praying for me. Help me keep interceding for my prodigal child. Teach me to pray like You. Amen.

MAKE IT PERSONAL

Ask another person to begin praying for your prodigal child. Ask them to commit to pray daily for the duration of this challenge.

Read Jesus' prayer in John 17. Make a list of His requests and begin praying through them for your child.

DIG DEEPER

When it comes to your prodigal, are you prayed out? When you can't find the words, pray God's Word back to Him. Pray through Psalm 27 today.

Day 9

ALL YOU NEED (GRACE NOTE)

by Ashley Gibson

TODAY'S READING: Psalm 23:1–3

The Lord is my shepherd;
I have what I need.
He lets me lie down in green pastures;
he leads me beside quiet waters.
He renews my life;
he leads me along the right paths
for his name's sake.
—Psalm 23:1–3

If the Lord is your Shepherd, take heart. He *will* give you rest. He *will* renew your life. He *will* lead you on for His glory. If the Lord is your Shepherd, you have all that you need.

"The Lord is my shepherd;
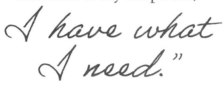
I have what I need."

Day 10

ONE THING I STILL WANT?

by Dan Jarvis

TODAY'S READING: Psalm 23:1

YOUR CHALLENGE:
Yield your desires to God, who loves you.

> The LORD is my shepherd;
> I shall not want.
> —Psalm 23:1 ESV

"But Lord, I really *do* want."

I want him to come home.
I want her to find her true identity in Christ.
I want our relationship to be restored.
I want the dinner table to be full again.

For every prodigal wandering life's highway, a mother, a wife, a daughter, a grandmother, or a friend is wondering if that lonely road will ever lead home.

Worrying. Wishing. Wanting.

And God our heavenly Father—our heavenly Shepherd—sees and knows every ache of the heart, every desire. In His great power, He could force a resolution; He could make the prodigals return all at once; He could push, pull, or press to get His way—and yours.

But for reasons known only to Him, He doesn't normally snap His fingers to accomplish His purposes. Instead, **He waits along with us. He tends to us; He provides for us; He stands with us. He plans rescue and redemption in ways we wouldn't.**

There's a bridge of faith you can cross today as you meditate on the Lord being your Shepherd. A bridge to trust, yielding not only your will to Him but your *wants* to Him.

It's difficult, to be sure. A mother sheep whose ewe has wandered away—what should she do? Break past the barriers herself and traverse the wilderness? Refuse her own care in futile protest? Or should she look up prayerfully to her Shepherd, just to be sure He knows (and He does). Will she trust His wisdom, His plan to invite rescue and return for the one she loves?

"The LORD is my shepherd."

He'll do what He must do, because His love is sure, His grace is abounding, His care is enough. That's all I want.

PRAY

Lord, I'm willing to want what You want. Everything in me wishes for this situation to change, for my loved one to return to You and the warmth of fellowship. I long for that. But You are my Shepherd, and that's enough for today. I choose to trust You.

MAKE IT PERSONAL

Have you decided to trust the Shepherd with the care of your prodigal?

How could you better demonstrate your trust in God when you discuss the situation with others?

DIG DEEPER

To encourage your heart toward contentment in the Lord alone, check out the *Revive Our Hearts* episode "God Is Enough." Find it at ReviveOurHearts.com/podcast.

Jesus waits along with you.

He tends to you; He provides for you;

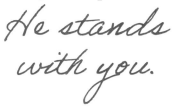

He stands with you.

Day 11

SOMEONE IS MISSING FROM THE GREEN PASTURE

by Dan Jarvis

TODAY'S READING: Psalm 23:2–3

YOUR CHALLENGE:
Believe that the same Shepherd who restored your soul can restore that of your prodigal.

> He makes me lie down in green pastures.
> He leads me beside still waters.
> He restores my soul.
> —Psalm 23:2–3 ESV

Gratefulness for the Shepherd's attentive care might fill your soul in a moment of worship or prayer: joy, fullness, expectation, even delight! But then, a *reminder*.

Someone is missing from this serene hillside, from the lush green grass and the peaceful watering hole. Other friends are here, yes, and perhaps other family members.

But it's not okay. "What about my prodigal?"

How can we enjoy being shepherded by the Lord Jesus when someone we love so much has walked away from Him? If only they could feel what we feel now; if only they could taste and see the goodness of the Lord.

They traded away all of this for what, exactly? How do we lie still in a green pasture when our prodigal could be in danger somewhere, even now? Or bask in the warmth of the spring sun while wondering if they are shivering somewhere, alone?

Once again, we turn our eyes to the Shepherd who brought us to this place of safety and delight. He planned to get us here, even "while we were still sinners" (Rom. 5:8). He made provision for us. Despite our rebellion, He graciously collected us and called us His own.

He can do the same for a prodigal. He always has room in His flock for one more.

And from this we draw hope: "He restores my soul." What He did for us, He can do for them. Even now He's glancing over the horizon, checking on the condition of prodigal hearts. He knows what it would take to bring them near.

He already went all the way to the cross on *their* behalf. Never forget that.

PRAY

Shepherd, it's so difficult to enjoy the fullness of faith and life when someone I care about is missing from the picture. It's like grief but different. Lord, I know You understand. You are no stranger to these emotions, watching so many that You love stray away. I know You love them, just as You loved me when I was lost.

WHILE YOU WAIT FOR YOUR *Prodigal*

MAKE IT PERSONAL

Have you been denying yourself the joys of green pastures, somehow believing you must wait for your prodigal to return first?

How does the Lord want you to handle this, and what direction can you receive from His Word?

DIG DEEPER

Would you like to learn how to find joy in the midst of suffering? Susan Hunt will guide you in the *Grounded* episode "Thriving in Joy with Susan Hunt." Find it at ReviveOurHearts.com/Grounded.

Day 12

GOD'S GRACE IS NOW AND FOREVER

by Dan Jarvis

TODAY'S READING: Psalm 23:3

YOUR CHALLENGE:
Plan on celebrating the grace of God.

> He leads me in paths of righteousness
> for his name's sake.
> —Psalm 23:3 ESV

Let's admit it: our human hearts are complicated.

Sometimes we mourn the loss our prodigal is experiencing, and sometimes we mourn *our* loss. What could have been; what should have been.

Deep down we suspect our prodigal's rebellion somehow reflects on us—our parenting, our planning, our lack of, well, *something*. **Something didn't go the way we expected, and we wonder if it's our fault.** "Have others noticed this? Do they suspect something too?"

Rather than judge such thoughts, let's just admit they are real.

Even God, perfect and holy, mentioned numerous times in the Old Testament that as His people rebelled against Him or turned aside to worship idols, it reflected poorly upon Him. Sure, there was real damage to the prodigal nation as a result of their choices, but there was also damage done to God's *reputation*. **When faced with this, God moved toward love, not regret. He sought first to redeem, showcasing His perfections not only through justice but through grace.**

So look again at our text today: why does our Shepherd lead us in paths of righteousness? Is it to clear our consciences of sin, to teach us the way of truth, to purify our hearts? Surely yes, and so much more! We benefit immensely from His mercy and direction. But notice another motive in the heart of the Shepherd: *"for his name's sake."*

His skill and care as a Shepherd, *His name*, somehow that's on the line.

To Him, our prodigal's heart isn't a passive concern. No, for us, and for His name's sake, He calls to them in the cold of the night. He searches among rocky outcroppings and along dusty, dangerous side trails. He beckons them to return to righteous pathways just as we do, likely *more than we do.*

In Ephesians, we read of the great salvation provided by Christ and the future trajectory of those He saves: He "raised us up with him and seated us with him in the heavenly places in Christ Jesus, so that in the coming ages he might show the immeasurable riches of his grace in kindness toward us in Christ Jesus" (Eph. 2:6–7 ESV).

In those coming ages, we will be living trophies of God's grace. Our concern then won't be on what our behaviors (or those of our prodigals) say about us but about what God's grace says about Him. What a day of rejoicing that will be!

PRAY

Jesus, I yield to Your wisdom and love. I know that Your name is on the line as well, as the Shepherd for [insert name]. You want to secure their return just as I do, and today I choose to believe that afresh.

MAKE IT PERSONAL

Have you been harboring concern about how your prodigal's choices reflect back on you or others you love?

Could you yield these cares to Jesus today?

DIG DEEPER

Listen to Nancy share about how to handle suffering in a way that brings God glory in the *Revive Our Hearts* episode "Perspective on Suffering." Find it at ReviveOurHearts.com/podcast.

Day 13

AS LONG AS JESUS IS NEAR

by Dan Jarvis

TODAY'S READING: Psalm 23:4

YOUR CHALLENGE:
Pray for your prodigal's awareness of God's presence.

> Even though I walk through the valley of the
> shadow of death,
> I will fear no evil,
> for you are with me;
> your rod and your staff,
> they comfort me.
> —Psalm 23:4 ESV

Is it cliché to imagine someone hitting rock bottom before they see the light?

Of course while our hearts break over our prodigals and their choices, we still wish for the best. We hope the natural consequences are not too severe; we hope the damage done isn't permanent. In the metaphor of Psalm 23, we hope the "valley of the shadow of death" does not lead them to death itself.

As we contemplate this metaphor, there are two possible images we construct. Both are relevant, but only one was intended by the psalmist.

The first image is that of a wandering sheep stumbling into such a valley by his own poor choices. He strayed from the flock, found himself in a tragic and dangerous situation, and now he needs a Luke 15-style rescue. The ninety-nine are secure in the green pasture, and a brave shepherd has set out to rescue this lost one.

This is certainly one way we pray for prodigals.

But Psalm 23 invites us to imagine another scenario—one in which the shepherd guides his beloved flock through the dark valley *on purpose*. Why? Because the next green pasture lies ahead. Because there is a source of water and rest just beyond the next bend.

Because the shepherd knows where he's going, even when the sheep doesn't.

The rod and the staff of the shepherd, used to direct and even lightly discipline sheep, keep them on the right path. Feeling the tap and pull of those tools gives a worried sheep confidence that they are still under his watchful care. As long as He is near enough to touch them in this way, there is no reason for fear.

Prayers of faith can recognize that the trials our prodigals are experiencing can be brought on by their loving Shepherd. A sheep may not feel grateful for the rod and staff; they may not enjoy the dark valley pathways, but they also may not realize what dangers lurk if they go their own way.

Prodigals may call out for relief from the discomfort that is really their best means of rescue. Rather than joining such calls by praying against hardship, let us pray instead that they sense the close presence of the Shepherd.

His nearness turns even the worst discomfort into a comfort—for the prodigal who finally sees and for the one at home who watches and waits.

PRAY

Dear Jesus, You are the Good Shepherd I choose to trust. My prodigal may be walking through dark valleys. I know You are there with them. But in this moment I want to ask You to let them sense Your presence in a felt way. Lord, would You reassure them that You are near?

MAKE IT PERSONAL

When have you experienced the "rod and staff" of the Shepherd guiding your life?

Is it possible that some of the consequences your prodigal is facing could be evidence of the same kind of divine guidance?

DIG DEEPER

Jesus is familiar with the valley, so lean into the comfort of His "rod and staff." For more encouragement, read the *Revive Our Hearts* blog post "You Have a Friend in the Valley." You can find it at ReviveOurHearts.com/blog.

Day 14

GOD'S PLAN IS MUCH, MUCH BETTER

by Dan Jarvis

TODAY'S READING: Psalm 23:5

YOUR CHALLENGE:
Accept that God is *for* you and *for* your prodigal.

> You prepare a table before me
> in the presence of my enemies;
> you anoint my head with oil;
> my cup overflows.
> —Psalm 23:5 ESV

The process to bring them home may be difficult.
The repentance required may be painful.
The journey through the dark valley may be unpleasant.
But then, *an overflowing cup*.

How assuring it is to know that our Shepherd's plan is better than ours. **He's not after temporary reform; He's after a soul-transforming revival and a restoration that is a worthy testimony to His divine power.** He's after a new kind of life that demonstrates grace and love in awe-inspiring ways, both on earth and in eternity.

And He's committed to the good of His sheep—no matter where they are, no matter how far they've roamed, no matter what hurtful things they've said or done.

He loves them, and He has a plan to redeem prodigals like us. And like the person we're praying for right now.

But will the plan succeed in this case?

We know such things aren't ours to see, not ahead of time at least. To the extent our prodigal's choices are involved in the answer, we may have our doubts. We may wonder if anything will turn the tide, if any amount of hardship will wake them up, if any expression of love will break through their hard shell.

But God has ways. And God has means. Think of what He can do and of what He wants to do.

- *By preparing a table*—He considers our prodigal's needs and plans ahead to meet them, not with scraps tossed to someone unworthy but with a feast prepared for someone richly loved.

- *In the presence of enemies*—even those who may have been involved in our prodigal's demise, those who tempted him or her away from faith, family, or fellowship. Even they will see what God can do.

- *Through anointing with oil*—He commissions our loved one to a new life and purpose, empowering them for a mission God would have, for the good works prepared in advance for them to do.

- *With an overflowing cup*—a life so abundantly full of joy that it begins spilling out toward others; a life rich in love, a life filled with the Holy Spirit.

These joyous things are what the Shepherd intends for your prodigal, praying friend. He is *for* them, in every way, just as He is *for* you.

WHILE YOU WAIT FOR YOUR *Prodigal*

PRAY

Good Shepherd, I call on You today on behalf of my prodigal, one whom I love and care for so much. You have a plan for them, Lord. You know them, You care for them, You see them right where they are. I pray that they would have a mighty testimony of Your favor someday. That as far as grace and blessing are concerned, their cup would overflow!

MAKE IT PERSONAL

Have you experienced the fullness of life that the Shepherd intends? In what ways?

Are you willing to pray with faith about the vision God has for your prodigal, even if it is beyond your understanding?

DIG DEEPER

To hear more about the joy and fullness of life in the midst of trials, listen to the *Revive Our Hearts* episode "You Anoint My Head with Oil." You can find this episode at ReviveOurHearts.com/podcast.

Day 15

HE WILL FOLLOW WHEN YOU CAN'T

by Dan Jarvis

TODAY'S READING: Psalm 23:6

YOUR CHALLENGE:
Rest well as God watches over your prodigal.

Surely goodness and mercy shall follow me all
the days of my life,
and I shall dwell in the house of the Lord forever.
—Psalm 23:6 ESV

You can *rest*.

It's tempting of course to worry—to leave the light on, to stay up late, to keep checking and hoping. But there's a moment when we have to, in faith, decide to rest.

The Lord Jesus asked, "Can any of you add one moment to his life span by worrying?" (Matt. 6:27). We won't add to the life of our prodigal either; not by that means.

And take heart: **resting doesn't mean neglecting. It doesn't mean forgetting. It just means believing.** It means being able to pray with confidence, then being able to yield your prodigal into the very capable hands of God.

We choose to believe God's plan will come to pass without our worrying and pacing, without our scheming and strategizing. We do all that in love, of course, with good intent. It's not always wrong to try our best, but there comes a moment when choosing to trust means choosing to entrust. *Could this be a moment like that for you?*

The goodness and mercy of God will follow your loved one even when you can't. When there isn't much news, when they haven't returned our call, when you aren't sure if they saw the message. When you aren't even sure where they are.

That's when we look up at our Shepherd again, as we have so many times before, and breathe a sigh of relief. Not because the struggle is over but because **it isn't our burden to carry. He knows, and He's watching.**

All of His goodness and mercy will follow our prodigals, even to the least desirable places. He won't give up; He won't stop; He'll keep watch. He'll keep calling their name, offering them rescue, giving them another chance.

And notice this: the psalmist knows God will be with him—that's half of the hope. But he also looks forward to *being with God*, not just for a moment but forever. Dwelling in God's house is not just about location, it's about fellowship. It's not just about an address, it's about a sense of belonging. And in hope, the prodigal we love can dwell with us again and, more importantly, in the house of the Lord forever. To that end, we pray.

PRAY

Lord, what a joyful reunion it will be, in this life or in the next, if [insert name] could just dwell with us again. I admit I've carried a burden that is too much for me, one that I can't sustain. Good Shepherd, I trust You. Would You keep watch and give rest to my weary soul?

MAKE IT PERSONAL

Read back through Psalm 23 again, thinking of your prodigal. But this time replace each first-person pronoun with his or her name. Recognize how much God loves them!

DIG DEEPER

To read more on giving your burden to the Lord, check out the *Revive Our Hearts* blog post "Take My Yoke and Learn from Me." Find it at ReviveOurHearts.com/blog.

Day 16

THE HOPE-FILLED PROMISES OF GOD (GRACE NOTE)

by Ashley Gibson

TODAY'S READING: Ezekiel 34:12

> As a shepherd looks for his sheep on the day he is among his scattered flock, so I will look for my flock. I will rescue them from all the places where they have been scattered on a day of clouds and total darkness.
> —Ezekiel 34:12

There has always been hope for God's people, even if they are scattered and in days of darkness. When you find yourself in need of a hearty dose of hope, rehearse to yourself the bountiful promises of God found in Scripture and let the Keeper of those promises sustain your heart.

THE HOPE-FILLED PROMISES OF GOD (GRACE NOTE)

Let the Keeper of those promises 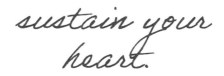 *sustain your heart.*

Day 17

FAR GREATER THAN FICTION

by Katie Laitkep

TODAY'S READING: Ezekiel 34:11–31

YOUR CHALLENGE:
Trust the unchanging character of God.

> "For this is what the Lord God says:
> See, I myself will search for my flock and
> look for them."
> —Ezekiel 34:11

When it comes to baby showers, my favorite trend is watching young mamas-to-be presented with stacks of picture books in lieu of cards. Many guests bring the books they cherished as children. Without fail, one title always appears multiple times since so many of us grew up hearing our own mothers read:

> I'll love you forever,
> I'll like you for always,
> As long as I'm living
> my baby you'll be.[1]

In the book, the baby grows up and gets a house across town. The scene that follows always made me giggle as a little girl. The mother hoists a ladder up to her adult son's bedroom window, climbs in, crawls across the floor, and once again makes him a promise the reader does not doubt for a second: "I'll love you forever." *I will, I will, I will.*

The fictional mama with a ladder strapped to the roof of her truck, who drives through the dark to get to her son, reflects the picture of the Lord presented in Ezekiel 34:11–31. As you read those verses, underline every time the Lord says, "I will." You'll find over twenty first-person promises such as the one in verse 11: "I myself will search for my flock."

[1] Robert Munsch, *Love You Forever* (Buffalo, NY: Firefly Books Ltd., 2004), 1.

Every promise in this passage gives insight into the Lord's character. **He is the God who is personally involved with His people and who takes action for their good. He's the Good Shepherd. A faithful Father.**

Do those characteristics feel fictional to you? Maybe you find it hard to believe the Lord truly cares about your prodigal or that He is intimately involved in your situation. Maybe you question if He really has the power to rescue the scattered. Rest in the assurance of His unchanging character. **As long as you're living (and beyond), He will remain the God who seeks the lost, brings back the strays, bandages the injured, and strengthens the weak (v. 16).**

PRAY

Lord, I'm so thankful that You are a God who is personally involved with His people. You fulfill every promise You make. Help me to trust that what Scripture reveals about You is true. May the unchanging reality of Your character be the foundation of my faith.

WHILE YOU WAIT FOR YOUR *Prodigal*

MAKE IT PERSONAL

Which attribute of God's character do you struggle to believe is true?

Choose one character trait and take a few minutes to thank Him for how it changes the way you are able to respond to your current situation.

DIG DEEPER

Learn more about how knowing the Lord makes a difference in how you respond to your circumstances on the *Grounded* episode "When You Cannot Trace the Plans of God, Trust the Character of God" with Ruth Chou Simons. Find it at ReviveOurHearts.com/Grounded.

Day 18

BRING THEM HOME

by Katie Laitkep

TODAY'S READING: Ezekiel 34:11–16

YOUR CHALLENGE:
Reflect on the rescue story God has written in your life.

> "I will rescue them from all the places where they have been scattered on a day of clouds and total darkness."
> —Ezekiel 34:12

Those who have raised teenagers recently have had one particular advantage over their predecessors: *tracking devices*. In today's world, as parents teach their teenagers to drive, they're able to turn on location features, making it easy to know where their child is when they venture off on their own for the first time. That information can bring some comfort to a mom's heart. But tracking an icon on a digital map doesn't bring the same peace as watching your loved one pull back into your driveway and knowing that he's home.

Ezekiel 34:11–16 is filled with descriptions of God Himself going out to get His sheep in order to bring them back: "I will rescue them from all the places," the Lord declared in verse 12. When His sheep were scattered, the dispersion event was characterized as "a day of clouds and total darkness" (v. 12).

You may be feeling as though you're living in a state of darkness as you face not only physical separation from your prodigal but emotional and spiritual distance. **If today your prodigal feels too far gone or if you're struggling to see through the clouds, consider how you have personally experienced God's rescue.**

If you are in Christ, you have already experienced the Lord's power to break the weight of your yoke and free you from the sin that enslaved you. As Colossians 1:13

says, "He has rescued us from the domain of darkness and transferred us into the kingdom of the Son he loves." Radical redemption is accomplished by His relentless pursuit.

The Lord is not done writing rescue stories. As you wait for your prodigal to return home, allow the Lord to restore your hope by reminding you that "you who were far away have been brought near by the blood of Christ" (Eph. 2:13).

PRAY

Lord, thank You for the redemption story You've already written in my life through Jesus. Only You are able to rescue us from the domain of darkness and to bring those who are scattered back from all the places they have gone. Bring my prodigal back to his own soil. Please, Lord, bring him all the way home.

WHILE YOU WAIT FOR YOUR *Prodigal*

MAKE IT PERSONAL

In what ways are you currently experiencing distance from your prodigal? Ask the Lord to help you believe that no distance is too great for Him to stretch out His hand and save.

How does reflecting on how the Lord has rescued you through Christ give you hope?

DIG DEEPER

Scripture is filled with stories portraying God's relentless pursuit to rescue and redeem. In the *Revive Our Hearts* season "Rahab and the Thread of Redemption," you'll hear the remarkable testimony of God's mercy in one of the most unlikely places.

Day 19

UNMASKING THE WOLVES

by Katie Laitkep

TODAY'S READING: Ezekiel 34:20–23
YOUR CHALLENGE:
Reflect on the Lord's role as Shepherd and as Judge.

> "I will establish over them one shepherd . . .
> He will tend them himself and
> will be their shepherd."
> —Ezekiel 34:23

You're likely familiar with the phrase "wolf in sheep's clothing." It's a metaphorical expression with biblical origins (see Matt. 7:15) that's made its way into many Hollywood scripts. A few years ago, I saw a superhero movie that introduced a new charismatic character in one of the opening scenes. When this new man appeared, he fought alongside the hero, helping him to victory. Not only did he seem to be a trustworthy ally, he also gained audience sympathy as he shared details of his traumatic past. Then came the plot twist. His mask came off, and his true identity was revealed. He wasn't a protagonist at all but a predator.

At the beginning of Ezekiel 34, the Lord unveiled the true identity of a group of corrupt shepherds who had taken advantage of the flock. Those shepherds should have led with strength and compassion. Instead, they had put their own interests first (v. 2), ruled with violence and cruelty (v. 4), and allowed the scattered sheep to become food for wild animals (v. 5).

Your prodigal may currently be influenced by a group of people that he trusts are on his side but that you can see are merely wolves in sheep's clothing. While it may be obvious to you that your prodigal is vulnerable to those taking advantage of him, perhaps you haven't been able to intervene.

The Lord knows those who have wronged your prodigal. In Ezekiel 34, we see that the Lord not only rescues His sheep, He also judges wrongdoing. Like the truest of heroes, He will ultimately not allow evil to prevail. "I will save my flock," the Lord declared. "They will no longer be prey, and I will judge" (v. 22).

As you seek the Lord for your prodigal, rest assured that **He is not only able to rescue the vulnerable but He will also hold accountable those who exploit and deceive.** Take comfort that the day will come when all evil will be defeated and the Lord's people will be safely restored under the just guidance of the one true Shepherd.

PRAY

Lord, I feel helpless when I see the ways that my prodigal is being influenced by people who don't have his best interest at heart. Help me to trust that You are in control, even now, and that You will not allow evil to prevail. Protect my prodigal so he is no longer prey, and allow him to find safety in the arms of the Good Shepherd.

MAKE IT PERSONAL

In what ways is your prodigal vulnerable to those around him? Ask the Lord to protect him from those who would take advantage of him.

Why does it matter that the Lord is not only a shepherd but a judge?

DIG DEEPER

There is no one else like Jesus. Get to know Him by joining Nancy DeMoss Wolgemuth on a 50-day journey in her book *Incomparable*. You'll consider the work and words of Christ and discover why there's none like Him.

Day 20

A COVENANT OF PEACE

by Katie Laitkep

TODAY'S READING: Ezekiel 34:25–31

YOUR CHALLENGE:
Thank the Lord for what the Good Shepherd has made possible.

> "I will make a covenant of peace with them and eliminate dangerous creatures from the land, so that they may live securely in the wilderness and sleep in the forest."
> —Ezekiel 34:25

He was the kid who heard you say the knife was sharp but didn't believe it until after he grabbed the edge with his tiny fist. She was the teenager who saw the warnings about strong currents and still made her way into the waves. They were the young adults who faced consequences that could have been avoided if they hadn't chosen the harder way.

This frustrating cycle is not new to our modern age. Throughout the Old Testament, the people of God were presented with options for how they were to live, and so often, they chose to take the harder path. In Deuteronomy 28, the Lord made a covenant with His people and told them that **if they obeyed Him, every aspect of their life would be blessed. But if they disobeyed Him, they would experience destruction, disease, drought, and defeat. You can predict how this turned out.**

In Ezekiel 34, the Lord promised to "make a covenant of peace" with His people, which would provide for them permanent security and safety from all enemies and opposition (v. 25). This new covenant is not contingent on the flock's perfect obedience but was made possible through the mercy and grace of the Messiah, the Good Shepherd who laid down His life for His sheep (John 10:11).

As a result of this permanent covenant, the Lord declared in Ezekiel 34:27 that His flock would be secure in their land. "They will know that I am the LORD when I break the bars of their yoke and rescue them from the power of those who enslave them."

Right now, the yoke your prodigal wears may be obvious to you but not to them. **Today, he or she may still be enslaved to sin and weighed down by suffering, but this does not have to be his future. May your prodigal, perhaps one who has often chosen a path that leads to slavery, come to know firsthand the freedom and safety made possible through Christ.**

PRAY

Lord, for every area of my prodigal's life where he has experienced the destruction from not following You, may he come to experience victory and flourishing in Christ. Please, Lord, will You break the yoke of sin and death and allow him to experience the freedom and deliverance that are possible for those who trust in You.

WHILE YOU WAIT FOR YOUR *Prodigal*

MAKE IT PERSONAL

Consider your own testimony. In what ways has your disobedience toward the Lord prevented you from experiencing His freedom? What have you learned about His mercy?

Write a prayer to the Lord thanking Him for His grace that has allowed you to experience true freedom in Christ.

DIG DEEPER

Those who are in Christ have been given true freedom. Find out more about what that means in the *Revive Our Hearts Weekend* episode "Freedom in Christ."

Day 21

THE NEARNESS OF GOD IN YOUR NEED

by Katie Laitkep

TODAY'S READING: Ezekiel 34:25–31

YOUR CHALLENGE:
Make a list of truths that have become increasingly precious to you.

> "Then they will know that I, the LORD their God, am with them, and that they, the house of Israel, are my people."
> —Ezekiel 34:30

There are aspects of Christianity that we can easily take for granted:

- We pray to a God who hears our prayers (1 John 5:14).
- We pray to a God who cares about our needs (Matt. 6:31–32).
- We pray to a God who is not limited by any difficulty (Jer. 32:17).

These may be statements that you've known for years in theory, but as a result of your journey with a prodigal, perhaps these realities are becoming more precious to you with every passing day. **With life as painful as it is, you can't afford to leave life-changing truths for Christmas morning and Easter Sunday. It's not enough to sing about Immanuel, "God with us," only during the holiday season. You need the Good Shepherd to be your ever-present help on the nights when your prodigal calls to give you bad news or when he breaks your heart by refusing to speak to you at all.**

God Himself spoke of the importance of realizing that He is near. In Ezekiel 34:30, as the Lord addressed His people, He said, "Then they will know that I, the Lord their God, am with them." Consider it: He is *God* with us. God *with* us. God with *us*.

But what if this were not the case? If He were a God who was absent, we'd have no reason to hope that all things are being worked out for good (Rom. 8:28). There would be no comfort in our affliction (2 Cor. 1:4). No companionship in our loneliness (Psalm 25:16). No provision of strength or grace when we're too weary to continue on (Isa. 40:31).

Praise God that we not only have a Savior who draws near to us now but One who promises even greater intimacy in eternity to come:

> Then I heard a loud voice from the throne: Look, God's dwelling is with humanity, and he will live with them. They will be his peoples, and God himself will be with them and will be their God. He will wipe away every tear from their eyes. Death will be no more; grief, crying, and pain will be no more, because the previous things have passed away. (Revelation 21:3–4)

PRAY

Lord, thank You for being a God who is near. Your promise to be with us brings hope, comfort, and strength. Remind me of Your presence and help me not to take it for granted.

MAKE IT PERSONAL

In what ways has the reality of God's nearness become more precious to you through your journey with your prodigal?

In what practical ways can you cultivate a greater awareness of God's presence in your daily life?

DIG DEEPER

"What does the coming of Immanuel mean to us?" Nancy DeMoss Wolgemuth says, "It means the end of captivity. It means we've been ransomed; we've been redeemed. It means the end of exile. We're no longer alienated. We're no longer separated from God and from one another." Hear more about what it means that God is with us in the *Revive Our Hearts* podcast episode "God with Us."

Day 22

"YOU ARE MY SHEEP"

by Katie Laitkep

TODAY'S READING: Ezekiel 34:25–31

YOUR CHALLENGE:
Allow the Lord to comfort you with the truth that you belong to Him.

> "You are my flock, the human flock of my pasture, and I am your God."
> —Ezekiel 34:31

Whether you're a mother, grandmother, sister, aunt, or friend, you have a unique relationship with your prodigal that keeps you committed to this challenge. Day after day, you're driven to your knees in prayer because of the personal bond you will always have. Your relationship may be strained, but the threads that tie you together remain.

Long before he walked away from your home, he was *your* child.
Long before she believed the lies of the enemy, she was *your* granddaughter.
Long before she betrayed your trust, she was *your* best friend.

As you've watched others make claim to your prodigal's attention and affection, you've likely felt that sense of possessiveness over your relationship.

You are mine. That's the sentiment the Lord ends His declaration with in Ezekiel 34. After all that His sheep have experienced, He reminds them why it is that He has promised to rescue and restore them. "You are my flock, the human flock of my pasture," He says in verse 31, "and I am your God."

The love and commitment you feel toward your prodigal—as deep as it is—still does not come close to the

love and devotion of God. *You* are His sheep. In the original language, the word is plural (translated "flock" in the CSB), addressing the group as a whole. But if you read this verse in the ESV, the word "sheep" is used. In English, that word could be singular or plural.

The Lord had a unique relationship with the people, the flock, of Israel. He also has a unique relationship to you: if you're in Christ, *you* are His sheep. Read verse 31 again, allowing the Lord to affirm *your* relationship to Him. Hear Him say: *You are mine . . . and I am your God.* No one can take you from His hands (John 10:28–29).

As you pray for your prodigal today, know that you are held in everlasting arms (Deut. 33:27). You're never alone and never forgotten (Heb. 13:5).

You are His sheep. And He is your God.

PRAY

Lord, help me to internalize the profound truth that I am Yours and that You are my God. May the assurance of Your unbreakable grip give me peace and help me to persevere.

MAKE IT PERSONAL

How does the reality of God's relationship with you change the way that you pray?

Look up Deuteronomy 33:27. Write the first sentence of this verse on a sticky note or card and place it somewhere you'll see it often.

DIG DEEPER

If you need a reminder of how the Lord holds you close, Susan Hunt's classic message "Don't Give Up on Your Modeling Career," given at a *Revive Our Hearts* conference, will encourage your heart. She'll remind you how sweet it is to be able to rest in the strong arms and faithful love of your heavenly Father. Find it at ReviveOurHearts.com/events.

Day 23

REST IN THE GOOD SHEPHERD (GRACE NOTE)

by Ashley Gibson

TODAY'S READING: John 10:11

"I am the good shepherd. The good shepherd lays down his life for the sheep."
—John 10:11

The Lord is your Good Shepherd. He does not leave you to fend for yourself. He provides for you, protects you, and cares for you *perfectly*. Rest in His perfect care today.

REST IN THE GOOD SHEPHERD (GRACE NOTE)

Jesus provides for you, protects you, and cares for you perfectly. *Rest in His perfect care today.*

Day 24

THERE'S A THIEF ON THE LOOSE

by Laura Elliott

TODAY'S READING: John 10:1–6

YOUR CHALLENGE:
Rejoice in the knowledge that the Good Shepherd relentlessly pursues His sheep.

"The one who enters by the gate is the shepherd of the sheep. The gatekeeper opens it for him, and the sheep hear his voice. He calls his own sheep by name and leads them out."
—John 10:2–3

"Armed robber at large downtown. Suspect considered armed and dangerous."

The news alert flashes across your phone. You normally wouldn't pay much attention, but today is different. Your teenage son is there—alone and unaware of the danger that could lurk around every corner. You have no way to reach him, to protect him. You feel utterly out of control.

We often feel this way about our prodigal loved ones, don't we? As if we're watching from afar as they walk blindly toward danger and we're powerless to warn them. Even if we could, would they listen?

Today's reading reminds us that **there is, in fact, a thief on the loose—one who has no business roaming the pasture but who slithered over the wall nonetheless.** But we often forget that the pasture's rightful owner, the One who enters through the gate and never loses sight of an inch of His territory (nor any intruder prowling within), watches over every sheep.

The Lord *is* the "shepherd of the sheep" (v. 2). What does this mean? **First, His sheep hear His voice.** They can attempt to block it out for a time, tuning their ears to the sound of the robber and his vile friends instead. But make no mistake: if they are *truly* His, ultimately, they will hear—and heed—the voice of the Shepherd.

Second, the Shepherd calls His sheep *by name*. It's tempting to make excuses for our prodigals . . . "Yes, what they're doing is wrong. But you don't know their story. Their trauma. Their grief." But God knows our prodigals intimately. He knows the razor-sharp edges of their stories, the things that have broken their hearts. And He will deal with them in perfect proportions of justice and mercy, compassion and accountability, discipline and love.

Finally, be encouraged that those the Shepherd calls, He leads. His sheep can't go anywhere that He hasn't walked before them. Of course God doesn't lead prodigals into sin, but He can (and does) lead sinners into and through deep, dark valleys, doing whatever it takes to bring them to the end of themselves, where they can see their need for Him most clearly.

Rather than being frightened by that possibility, rejoice in the knowledge that the Good Shepherd pursues His sheep relentlessly and will stand for nothing less than their restoration to His fold.

PRAY

*Lord, thank You for Your loving care of Your sheepfold. I'm so grateful that nothing happens, within or without, that is outside of Your control. Though I plead for Your protection of my loved one, please use **whatever means You deem necessary** to bring [insert name] to Yourself. I need Your strength to pray "whatever it takes, Lord." Please help me to trust You today.*

MAKE IT PERSONAL

"Whatever it takes" feels like a dangerous prayer. Have you been afraid to pray it for your prodigal? Ask for God's help to pray boldly, trusting Him to pursue His sheep relentlessly and with compassion.

DIG DEEPER

Listen to the *Revive Our Hearts* podcast episode "He Is the Good Shepherd." Nancy DeMoss Wolgemuth will remind you that Jesus is the Good Shepherd because:

- His character is good.
- His motives are good.
- His methods are good.
- His skill is good.
- His heart for His sheep is good.
- His track record is perfect.

Day 25

FOR ABUNDANT LIFE, ENTER HERE

by Laura Elliott

TODAY'S READING: JOHN 10:7–13

YOUR CHALLENGE:

Preach the gospel to yourself. Preach it to your prodigal. Then pray.

> "I am the gate. If anyone enters by me, he will be saved and will come in and go out and find pasture."
> —John 10:9

"Sorry, I have a flock to protect," my hobby farmer friend said when another friend wondered aloud whether the "cute baby foxes" under her porch would be a problem if she got chickens. The farmer told her plainly that if he found foxes—baby or otherwise—on his property . . . let's just say they wouldn't be there long. These predators have one goal: to kill and eat the animals that are smaller or slower than they are.

Yesterday we read some bad news—that predators lurk in God's pasture as well. In today's reading, we learn their dark purpose: **"A thief comes only to steal and kill and destroy"** (v. 10). When danger comes to the pasture, not even the hired hand can be counted on to rescue the sheep, leaving them to be snatched up instead (v. 12). "This happens," Jesus said, "because he . . . doesn't care about the sheep" (v. 13).

Is your loved one counting on a "hired hand"—a sinful lifestyle, an unbiblical identity, their intellectual prowess, or independent spirit—to bring them peace and security? One day they'll see that ideologies and lifestyles make terrible farmhands, leaving them vulnerable and alone when it counts. Like fluffy foxes waiting to pounce, the twin thieves of Sin and Pride have only one goal: destruction.

A "hired hand" won't rescue them. *But Jesus can*. He yearns to. That's why He reminds us, "I am the good shepherd. I know my own, and my own know me ... I lay down my life for the sheep" (vv. 14–15). **In contrast to the thief who is out for blood, Jesus gave His blood so we "may have life and have it in abundance" (v. 10).**

There's one caveat to His protection: they must enter through Jesus, the gate (v. 9). Whoever enters by Him "will be saved and will come in and go out and find pasture." It's an ironclad guarantee.

However, the reverse is also true. If anyone *has not* entered through Him, they will not be saved. These sheep don't hear the voice of the Shepherd but the deceptive din of thieves and robbers instead (v. 8). It's a heartbreaking reality: **some of those whom we pray will return home are not yet in the fold.**

Perhaps you're thinking of your dear one now. Wondering, hope against hope, whether it's the Savior or the serpent they hear. **Take comfort: your job is not to be the arbiter of their soul.** God is the Judge whose verdicts are faithful and true. Your job is simple: preach the gospel to yourself. Preach the gospel to your prodigal. And pray. Oh, how we must pray!

The Shepherd is eagerly, lovingly, joyfully adding to His flock still today.

PRAY

Lord Jesus, whom have I to turn to but You? I don't know the heart of my loved one, but You do. You see clearly and judge rightly. You are always, only good. If [insert name] doesn't truly know You as Lord and Savior, may today be the day [he/she] repents and believes. If [he/she] has simply strayed, let Your voice be undeniable. Bring repentance and restoration. Help me to remember that I need the gospel every day. Help me be bold in proclaiming it in word and deed, as I interact with [insert name] and others.

MAKE IT PERSONAL

Prodigals aren't alone in being blind to the danger of sin. Are there "fluffy foxes" you've allowed in your life, waiting for the opportunity to cause your faith to wobble? Make a plan to shoo them out through confession, repentance, and spending time in God's Word.

DIG DEEPER

In her blog post, Stacey Salsbery invites you to "Persevere in Preaching the Gospel to Yourself." She'll help you remember why the gospel isn't only for the unsaved . . . why we all need it every day. Find it at ReviveOurHearts.com.

Day 26

JESUS KNEW THEN WHAT HE KNOWS NOW

by Laura Elliott

TODAY'S READING: JOHN 10:14–21
YOUR CHALLENGE:
Thank God for knowing you—and your prodigal—completely.

> "I am the good shepherd. I know my own, and my own know me, just as the Father knows me, and I know the Father. I lay down my life for the sheep."
> —John 10:14–15

If I only knew then what I know now . . .

How many times have you heard this phrase? (Or even used it yourself?) The shiny car with a price tag to match that turned out to be a lemon . . . the time you procrastinated on a project and then came down sick the day before the due date . . . when you saw your grandma, not knowing it was the last time, but didn't give her a kiss goodbye . . . when the relationship that began with butterflies and promises ended in gut-wrenching betrayal.

If you only knew then what you know now . . .

What's the underlying sentiment? Usually it's "I would have done things differently" or, in some cases, not at all. Not so with our Savior.

"I am the good shepherd," He said. "I know my own and my own know me" (John 10:14). The word *know* here is serious. This isn't some vague acquaintance like I might say I know someone I met one time at a party. This is deep, intimate knowledge. Jesus compares it to the way He knows the Father and the Father knows Him (v. 15).

Jesus' knowledge of you comes with a built-in eternal timeline. That means when He willingly laid down His life for you and me, He knew every time we would run from Him, lie to Him, deny Him, do exactly what He told us *not to* do, and willfully neglect what He told us *to* do. He knew we would mock Him, spit on Him, and betray Him in every way imaginable. He knew our sin would lead Him to the cross.

He knew then what we know now. **And He laid down His life for His sheep anyway,** picked it up again three days later, defeating death, hell, and all the powers of evil, and secured for eternity our privileged position in His pasture.

Praying friend, if you're grieving over your prodigal's sin today, remember that on the cross Jesus grieved over your sin too. It was just as heinous. Just as offensive. Just as much a betrayal as theirs. And He rescued you anyway. **Hang onto the hope that one day your loved one's eyes will be reopened to the wonder of Jesus' sacrifice, that he or she will repent and experience the joy of restoration. Oh, what a day that will be!**

They'll know then what we know now. Hallelujah!

PRAY

Lord, thank You for not giving up on me when You knew how often I'd run from You. Thank You for sending Your Son, Jesus, to die on the cross for my sin in spite of the countless ways I've sinned against Him, before salvation and since. I pray that You would show mercy to [insert name] in the same bounteous way You have shown it to me. Open their eyes, Lord. Help them to know You as I do, that together we can exalt You, our gentle, holy, perfect Shepherd.

MAKE IT PERSONAL

Jesus knows you intimately and completely, but there's no end to getting to know Him. Have you thanked Him for being infinite? Take time to do so now.

DIG DEEPER

Linger a little longer on the fact that you and the whole world—from the macro to the micro—are fully known by Jesus, as you listen to "Jesus Knows You," an episode of the *Revive Our Hearts* podcast.

Day 27

UNSNATCHABLE

by Laura Elliott

TODAY'S READING: JOHN 10:22–30

YOUR CHALLENGE:
Believe that what belongs to God is His forever.

> "I give them eternal life, and they will never perish. No one will snatch them out of my hand."
> —John 10:28

An English proverb says, "Hell hath no fury like a woman scorned." As a mother of six, I say hell hath no fury like a little boy who wants his brother's new toy. You've seen it before. It's the younger sibling's birthday, and big brother is not a fan. "Wow," my son said, eyes wide, when he saw his brother's present. "I've never seen a bike like *that* before . . ."

From that moment on, he could think of nothing else (including his own bike). He wanted to ride *that* bike and was willing to do just about anything—from whining to conniving—to get it. He even pretended to be immensely interested in one of the other gifts in a shrewd attempt to lure the birthday boy away so he could snatch up the bike. But it wasn't going to happen; in our house, we had a rule: on your birthday, you had exclusive rights to your new gift unless you chose to share. No one could take it away.

In the Shepherd's pasture, a similar but far more binding order is in force. In fact, in just a few sentences (vv. 27–30), Jesus recited a whole series of promises:

- "My sheep hear my voice."
- "I know them, and they follow me."
- "I give them eternal life."
- "They will never perish."

- "No one will snatch them out of my hand."

- "My Father, who has given them to me, is greater than all."

- "No one is able to snatch them out of the Father's hand."

- "I and the Father are one."

Jesus was building an argument about who He is based on His relationship with the Father, and its climax was that no one—NO ONE—(notice He said it twice) can snatch away what's His.

Do you worry that the world or the devil or some other evil has snatched away your prodigal's faith and, with it, their salvation? Be not afraid. If they are His sheep, then no one, *nothing*, can snatch them out of His hand. If He has given them eternal life, not even a decade of poor choices can mess it up.

The greater danger is, as Jesus answered His critics in verse 26: "But you don't believe **because you are not of my sheep.**" Our prodigal loved ones will never be snatched from His hand. But we must first pray that they indeed belong to Him. For those that don't, may this be the day their eyes are opened—that they inherit the promise of being permanently, truly unsnatchable.

PRAY

Oh, Father, thank You for being both the hand that is always open to Your own and utterly unbreachable to those who would snatch what's Yours. Thank You that our salvation is shored up with Your promises—guaranteed and good forever. Help me to trust You to keep Your Word.

MAKE IT PERSONAL

Do you hesitate to doubt your prodigal's childhood profession of faith out of fear that your suspicions might be true? Like cancer spreading unrestrained because we're afraid to go to the doctor, bringing the symptoms out into the light is the first step toward healing. If you suspect your loved one is unredeemed, recruit a team of friends to storm the throne room of heaven on their behalf, asking the Lord to bring conviction and open their eyes as only He can. Then remember that He loves them more than you ever could and will only do right by them.

DIG DEEPER

Have you believed the lie that your child's salvation depends on you? Shannon Popkin can relate. Find out how she battles against that lie in the blog post "You Can Trust God with Your Child's Salvation." Find it at ReviveOurHearts.com.

Day 28

EQUIPPED FOR ADVERSITY

by Laura Elliott

TODAY'S READING: JOHN 10:31–39

YOUR CHALLENGE:
Follow Jesus' example when you're under fire.

"But if I am doing [my Father's works] and you
don't believe me, believe the works.
This way you will know and understand that
the Father is in me and I in the Father."
—John 10:38

Scripture records it so casually you could almost miss it:

> Again the Jews picked up rocks to stone him.
> (John 10:31)

Surely the hearts of His critics were beating wildly as their hands grasped cold, hard stones. Jesus remained calm. He asked good questions, questions that ultimately revealed that it wasn't the things He had done that fueled their rage. It was His message. "Because you—being a man," they said, "make yourself God" (v. 33). They had accused Him of other things, from healing on the Sabbath to demon possession and more, but this time at least they were being honest. It was His message not His methods they objected to.

Have you encountered adversity as you've attempted to speak truth to your prodigal? Have you been accused of being unloving, backward, or bigoted? Of abandonment or pushing your loved one away?

First, evaluate your heart. It may be true that you have sinned against your loved one with unkind speech, dishonesty, anger, an unwillingness to listen, or a prideful heart. If God reveals any wicked way in you, repent and seek forgiveness. But if your conscience is clean, **remember that in the case of Jesus' critics, it wasn't Him but His message that was offensive. As the apostle Paul reminded us, "The word of the cross is**

foolishness to those who are perishing, but it is the power of God to us who are being saved" (1. Cor. 1:18).

Jesus used the Word of God, which His accusers wouldn't argue with, to ask the next logical question, pointing them toward the unavoidable truth that He is the Son of God (vv. 34–36). But He also gave them an alternative: if "you don't believe me, believe the works. This way you will know and understand" (v. 38).

You too can use God's Word to help point your prodigal to the inevitable conclusion of who Jesus is and why they desperately need to return to Him. **But you have another tool in your arsenal: His work in you.** Sharing winsomely and honestly about how God is at work in your heart and life, even through this trial, is truth they cannot deny—because it's the reality of Christ in you, the hope of glory.

PRAY

Jesus, when faced with conflict or challenges to my faith, help me to respond as You did: with composure and clarity. May Your ever-powerful Word and Your humbling work in my life testify to the sweetness of walking with You. I pray for [insert name] now, that [he/she] would be disarmed by Your love and that our next conversation would be the first step in their journey back toward You.

MAKE IT PERSONAL

Consider all that God has done in your heart through this trial with your prodigal. Start a list and thank Him for each entry, even those parts that are painful.

DIG DEEPER

Conflict is never easy. The episode of the *Grounded* videocast "A Right Theology of Christian Conflict, with Mark Vroegop" will help you learn to use it as a gospel opportunity. Find it at ReviveOurHearts.com/Grounded.

Day 29

ACROSS THE JORDAN

by Laura Elliott

TODAY'S READING: JOHN 10:40–42

YOUR CHALLENGE:
Rest in the knowledge that Jesus knows exactly what they need.

> Many came to him and said, "John never did a sign, but everything John said about this man was true." And many believed in him there.
> —John 10:41–42

We didn't know he was autistic yet, just that he was a little "behind." Our third son was three and a half years old, and it felt like he was by my side every waking moment. One day I realized why: I was nearly the only person that could understand a word he said. I was his mom . . . *and* his interpreter. Soon the severity of the problem became evident, and the more I thought about it, the more I lamented: how could speaking simple words, something that came so easily to every other toddler I knew (including my first two sons), be so painfully difficult for my little boy?

He began to see a wonderful speech therapist who had the knowledge and ability to help him, and soon his speech began improving. Finally others could understand him, and a new world began to unfold.

Perhaps you've been trying unsuccessfully to break through to your loved one for years—for decades even. It's discouraging, isn't it? Does it feel like you're not even speaking the same language, or do you wonder why the faith that feels so natural to others is so foreign to them? I wonder if that's how John felt while preaching in the wilderness (Matt. 3:1–11). He spoke truth and did the work that God had set before him, but in the end, it wasn't John or John's baptism the people needed. They needed someone who could not just baptize but save them. They needed an encounter with the Living Word.

Once Jesus crossed the Jordan "to the place where John had been baptizing earlier," something extraordinary occurred. "Many came to him and said, 'John never did a sign, but everything John said about this man was true.' **And many believed in him there**" (John 10:41–42).

Praying friend, don't be discouraged if your witness and words of biblical encouragement seem to be falling on deaf ears. Even if it feels like you're not speaking the same language as your prodigal, **it could be that your job is simply to prepare the way for Jesus to work in their life in a way that only He can.** May they one day realize that everything you said about Jesus was true . . . and *come home.*

PRAY

Father, thank You for using me as an instrument in Your kingdom and specifically in the life of [insert name]. Help me continue to pray diligently and speak truth with clarity, kindness, and compassion, remembering that only You can open their eyes to truth. You are the Shepherd, and we are the sheep. I long to see Your glory in the life of my loved one and eagerly await that day when Your name is lifted high, with every knee bowed and every tongue confessing that You, oh God, are Lord. May You receive all of the honor and praise, forever and ever. Amen.

MAKE IT PERSONAL

John said, "He must increase, but I must decrease" (John 3:30). You won't likely move to the wilderness to preach the gospel and eat locusts and honey, but what can you do today to die to yourself, making room for Christ to be magnified in your life?

DIG DEEPER

Much of John's time was spent calling sinners to repentance. But isn't that kind of negative? Nancy DeMoss Wolgemuth explains in the *Revive Our Hearts* podcast episode "Is It Loving to Call Someone to Repentance?" that the call to repentance is not a negative call. Instead, it's the most positive call in the world.

Day 30

HE'D LEAVE THE 99

CONCLUSION

by Erin Davis

Jesus' parable of the prodigal son is a famous one; perhaps you've turned to it often as you've waited to see your prodigal come home. Look again at that passage of Scripture and you'll see that Jesus told it with sheep in mind.

Luke 15 records that the Pharisees and scribes were sickened that Jesus dared to dine with sinners. Perhaps your own heart has felt disgusted at times at the sinful life your prodigal has chosen. Such reactions come naturally to people of flesh like us. Still Jesus calls your heart higher. He asks you to see your prodigal as the precious sheep they are.

> So [Jesus] told them this parable: "What man among you, who has a hundred sheep and loses one of them, does not leave the ninety-nine in the open field and go after the lost one until he finds it? When he has found it, he joyfully puts it on his shoulders, and coming home, he calls his friends and neighbors together, saying to them, 'Rejoice with me, because I have found my lost sheep!' I tell you, in the same way, there will be more joy in heaven over one sinner who repents than over ninety-nine righteous people who don't need repentance. (Luke 15:3–7)

Though your prodigal has busted through the fences God has lovingly placed in their life, His love for them is not diminished. He seeks out the lost. He desires to carry them home. He is able to woo your loved one away from the jaws of distress. He's done it before. He can and will do it again and again.

Take comfort in this image today: your wayward one carried on the broad shoulders of Jesus. Perhaps you saw glimmers of hope during this 30-day challenge. Maybe your prodigal did a full 180-degree turn and is now running toward the Lord instead of away from Him. Maybe your loved one's heart seems as hard as it did on Day 1 of this challenge. Be steadfast. Your hope is not in what your eyes can see but in the God who says, "Rejoice with me, because I have found my lost sheep!" (v. 6).

Keep praying for your prodigal. Keep trusting the Lord to call them back to Himself. Like the father in the parable of the prodigal son, keep watching the horizon. Today may be the day God brings your loved one home.

AUTHOR BIOS

Erin Davis is a writer and teacher passionately committed to getting women of all ages to the deep well of God's Word. She is the author of more than a dozen books and Bible studies, including *Lies Boys Believe*, *7 Feasts*, and *Fasting & Feasting*. Erin serves as the content director for *Revive Our Hearts* and hosts the *Women of the Bible* podcast and *Grounded* videocast. Hear her teach on *The Deep Well with Erin Davis* podcast. When she's not writing, you can find Erin chasing chickens and children on her small farm in the Midwest.

"Worthy is the Lamb who was slain,
to receive power and wealth and wisdom and might
and honor and glory and blessing!"
—Revelation 5:12 ESV

AUTHOR BIOS

Laura Elliott is a wife, mom of six, writer, editor, and serves as marketing content manager at *Revive Our Hearts*. God's Word, good coffee, and hot saunas warm her heart during cold Minnesota winters.

> Then we, your people, the sheep of your pasture,
> will thank you forever;
> we will declare your praise
> to generation after generation. —Psalm 79:13

Ashley Gibson is a native of the mountains of Maryland, lover of flowers, and an ardent believer in writing letters. Ashley serves as the social media content specialist for *Revive Our Hearts*. She lives in central Ohio with her husband, Collin, and loves encouraging others to know and love God deeply.

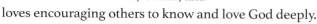

> "I am the good shepherd. I know my own, and my own know me." —John 10:14

Dan Jarvis is an author, speaker, and content strategist for *Revive Our Hearts*. He and his wife, Melissa, parent ten children, six of whom they adopted through foster care. Dan also serves as a local church pastor in Southwest Michigan.

> For you were like sheep going astray, but you have now returned to the Shepherd and Overseer of your souls. —1 Peter 2:25

Katie Laitkep was working as a hospital teacher when God called her to join *Revive Our Hearts* as a staff writer. She serves remotely from Houston, Texas, where God sustains her through saltwater beaches, Scripture, and her local church.

> For the Lamb who is at the center of the throne will shepherd them;
> he will guide them to springs of the waters of life,
> and God will wipe away every tear from their eyes.
> —Revelation 7:17

Revive Our Hearts™

Calling Women to Freedom, Fullness, and Fruitfulness in Christ

Daily Teaching | Events | Digital Media

Resources | Broadcast Media

For additional teaching from Nancy DeMoss Wolgemuth visit

ReviveOurHearts.com

Your Trustworthy Source for Biblical Truth

Don't let bitterness have the last word.

Move from Hurt to Hope

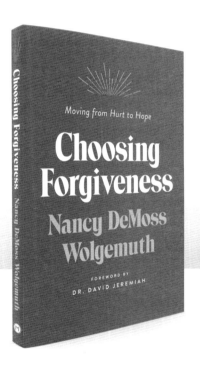

Nancy DeMoss Wolgemuth gives you practical, biblical principles straight from the pages of God's Word that can help you **surrender your bitterness** and **move toward hope.**

ReviveOurHearts.com